# EFFORTLESS

In a world of infinite possibilities what will you choose?

## by Evelyn McAleer

# EFFORTLESS

This book was first published in Great Britain in paperback during March 2020.

The moral right of Evelyn McAleer is to be identified as the author of this work and has been asserted by her in accordance with the Copyright, Designs and Patents Act of 1988.

In memory of my Mother, you will always be the Rose
that reminds me of why I do what I do. x

EVELYN MCALEER

# About Evelyn McAleer

Evelyn is a Spiritual life coach a motivational speaker, dance instructor and mother to three wonderful children that have inspired her in their own unique way with the many lessons teenagers can bring to home life.

"When you open your eyes every morning with a sense of purpose with a happiness at what you are doing and an excitement for what is to come that's a great life. Bring joy to the lives of others and in return you receive so much joy into your own life, that is the reason I dance every day with people ranging from 4 years old to 84 years old. Do what makes your heart sing"

**www.evelynmcaleer.com**

# CONTENTS

# ACKNOWLEDGEMENTS

I wish to acknowledge my gratitude to Erinrose who has shared the journey with me from conception to completion of this book. A beautiful young lady I am proud to call my daughter. Always dream your dream Erinrose, don't get caught up in drama and carry your wonderful smile with you throughout your life time. To my sons Micheál & Conor, thank you boys for the journey we have shared thus far in life, it's been pretty adventurous. Life can be challenging at a young age try to remember manifesting is always at work, keep the thoughts on what you want and be patient, you will receive what you put out. I love you all very much.

Thank you Mark Stephens for permitting me to share your toothbrush story, it has been a pleasure working with you. Steve & Don at the publishing company thank you gentlemen for everything you do. Thank you Adrian Morrison for your gift of photography for my cover. Jeff O'Driscoll M.D & Author thank you for your time our many conversations and your beautiful review. Jeffery C Olsen Author thank you for just being. I am blessed our paths crossed what an effortless connection where wonders awakened. Thank you for the time you gave to me.

# FOREWORD

As a child, I was told the biblical story of Jesus walking on the water. I was also told of how Jesus invited his friend Peter to join him. And how Peter actually did walk on the water for a moment, but then became fearful and sank. As I've grown older I have contemplated this story many times and found layers of deeper meaning within it. First of all, we are all invited to experience our divinity and walk on water. Jesus was not showing off, but knew Peter had the power to perform miracles as well. As do we all. Peter on the other hand, contrary to popular belief, was not walking by faith. He had already taken a few steps on top of the water. He knew he could do it. In fact he already was doing it. He simply began to doubt himself. Perhaps he even wondered if he 'should' be walking on water. The ego tends to do that sometimes. In fact often it whispers, "Who do you think you are? Get back in line like everyone else. How dare you step into your magnificence and your personal divinity. People who do that often get crucified. Don't turn water to wine. Behave!" - And thus we sink back into the small and ordinary lives we have created for ourselves. Playing the victim of our circumstances rather than being the creators of the lives we choose.

I have not yet mastered walking on water, but I have learned to swim. I also recall as a child flopping into the pool and thrashing violently in the fear of sinking and going under. The more I fought it, the faster I sank. It was not until I 'let go' and relaxed that I realized I could float. It was effortless if I only allowed it. Now, when I slip into the pool, I navigate the water with grace, rather than frantic thrashing. Experience has taught me this, to the point it has now become graceful instinct. I don't think about how to hold my breath or move my body and there is absolutely no fear of sinking. It truly is my natural state. I could float for hours if I chose, simply by trusting myself. It is effortless.

Life can be this way. The more we fight it, the more we thrash and panic, the deeper we seem to go. So deep at times it seems we are unable to breath or see or function with any kind of grace at all. Merely surviving. Drowning if you will in the victimhood we have chosen to experience our lives as. Stop! Stand up! Breath! The water may only be waste deep anyway. Choose to rise above the drama and see things with a higher perspective. And when the challenges do run deep, so deep there seems to be no bottom and standing up is not an option, (I've been there) if I stop, relax, trust, and fill my lungs with air, I float gracefully. And even more interestingly, the waves take me right where

I wanted to be in the first place. Trust, intension and committed action. That is what creates miracles.

Einstein, Anka, Bashar, a handful of brilliant minds have been attributed to quoting something to the effect of, "Everything is energy and that's all there is to it. Match the frequency of the reality you want and you cannot help but get that reality. It can be no other way. This is not philosophy. This is physics." My mind has simplified this for my own comprehension to, "You can only get to where you're coming from." In other words, if you want to experience peace, then exude peace. If you want to experience light, then shine light. If you want to experience love, then be love, in every aspect of your existence. This all takes so much effort you may say, however this is simply our conditioning. The truth is you are already all of these things. You are a unique manifestation of the divine, you came from that and are now showing up as only you can, with your unique vibration and unique tone in the great big universe, uni-verse, one song.

Ms. Evelyn McAleer has captured within the pages of EFFORTLESS an inspiring 'how to' guide including profound examples of how to be a powerful creator in this world by simply being you. Trusting, taking action and knowing you will manifest what you choose in your life as if you already have it.

As you read the following pages I invite you to open up and truly let it sink in. Try it and see, "Walk on the water Peter" - fear and doubt are the only things holding you back. Trust and love will see you through and you will begin to experience miracles. As you do, be aware that the most profound miracle you may experience could actually be you. You just may step into your magnificence and divinity in such a way to see miracles every day in the simple things; in every sunrise, in every blade of grass, in every whisper of the wind, and perhaps even in the mirror. After all, you are the miracle. "For blessed are the pure in heart, for they shall see God…" in everything and everyone. Including yourself.

*By Jeffery C. Olsen, Best-Selling Author of KNOWING*

## 'EFFORTLESS'

### Requiring no physical or no mental exertion

How I believe it is achievable

- Total trust in the divine nature of your existence and the divine source which you are of.

- Do what brings you joy.

- Letting go of having to control others and situations. Remember the only thing you are in control of are your own thoughts, words, actions and how you choose to experience everything in this life.

- Belief – When I went to pen the word belief the spelling was coming out all wrong. I tried writing it three times and then I looked at the letters that flowed effortless BELIFE just BE LIFE.

- Step away and let go of all that does not serve you, thoughts, feelings all situations and relationships whether that is with people, food, alcohol and the relationship you have with yourself.

- Change the way you see things. If the way you

are choosing to see situations is not serving you it is up to you to re-examine and change the way you are seeing it. Remember there are many sides to the coin, never permit ego to hold you in your steadfast thinking of old.

- Spend time in nature.

- Take time each day for yourself and your connection with the divine within you and surrounding you.

- Know that every person in your life who has wronged you, loved you, made you feel great or not so great are your teachers not punishers. There are no bad or awful experiences there are many experiences we wish not to relive again and many we would love one more chance to experience, but like everything in this life they to have passed it is only the feeling and memory you choose to carry with you. They are what they are please learn and grow from every experience then bring forth your wisdom and knowledge from your heart to help serve others.

- Your divine energy is eternal. Your true nature can never die it is only the form (your body) that has an expiry date.

- Never compare yourself to others. Know that you are connected to everything and everyone, you chose to come here with your gift, your passion, your talent. Some have forgotten why they are here, but know this you are the most precious creation, you have a unique gift to this world that only you deliver with your uniqueness.

As I sit down today to make a start on my second book I pray that every word I put to paper will be from my heart and flow effortless. As in my first book 'A Life You Want' my wish for you through reading is that you will connect with my heart, that you will connect with your magnificence, that you will remember that which you are off. Today as I commence my book marks the beginning of something new and also a very special date as my second child Mícheál officially becomes an adult at eighteen years old, the twin who made the miraculous journey to this world.

Every day is a new beginning a new start to the rest of your life. Today you get the choice how to begin the rest of your life. What will you do today that screams to the world

### I AM READY!

What dreams have been lying dormant within you?

I have no plan on the length of this book or how long it will take for completion I will allow myself to be guided and I will know when I have done enough for I am certain that I am enough. I have no expectations and a non attachment to the outcome I will let the outcome form itself. Whomever the book is to reach it will find its way there. Vision, feeling, belief and inspired action. No matter what you want to do firstly create the vision, get the feeling that it has already happened, believe that everything will unfold in divine time, the right people the right opportunities, the money it will all come in the unfolding and lastly take some inspired action. Inspired action is effortless, it is what your heart is calling you to do and even though your thoughts may be telling you otherwise always follow what your heart is asking of you, for that is your divine gift to this world. Today is my day of inspired action I believe the book is already created and the rest will just flow effortless.

The reason I have called the book 'effortless' I believe that is how all of the joys and love and wonders enter our lives, there is no force required, there is no doubt and all we require is to master patience. Yes there are many times when life gets difficult and feels like an unbearable struggle, times you want to hide from the world and not face what is ahead of you, but then you take that one precious deep breath and you face what has to be done by changing that one thought from what I 'have' to do to what I 'get' to do, it changes everything. Many of us come out the other side and when we look back it's only but a memory and feeling. If we have to constantly fight to keep something in our lives perhaps it's time to let it go or let go of the fight within you and deal with it another way. It is how you choose to see every single situation and how you wish to experience it will determine how effortless you move on. Look at how effortless nature and other species exist in this life. The trees do not worry about where they will receive nourishment in order to grow, the river does not concern itself whether it will rain or not to sustain the life that lives beneath and the billions of humans that depend on it. The birds do not lose sleep where their new home will be. Everything and every existence apart from humans live and breathe effortless they know that all will be delivered, that everything is in divine order. That is why I have chosen nature as my cover for the book, the next time you are out for a walk or a run or a cycle remove your headsets listen to the multitude of conversations taking place listen to the relaxing sounds of the water watch the birds in flight imagine just spending one day that is effortless and all that is required from you is just breathe be one with nature for that short time absorb your senses with the beauty that surrounds you. Become Effortless.

Throughout this book I will share experiences I have personally had or others whom I have had the privilege to call my clients. My wish is that some or all of these stories will resonate with you. If you are finding that life is an effort are you willing to begin seeing and thinking a different way to bring about an effortless life?

# *The Toothbrush*

I waited patiently on this chapter to manifest, a beautiful story of when we take inspired action, let go of what no longer serves us and believe in what we want to take place in our lives that it will all happen effortless. The beauty is that you do not need to be clear on every single thing all at once, your clarity will unfold with every new step you take on the path of your purpose. Mark came to me in April of 2019 as I type this is now the final week of November 2019, I have no doubt the following months of Marks life will bring only more joy and love in his life if he continues to carry out his daily practices of gratitude and meditation.

Mark was in the final months of his forty ninth year he felt now was the time to start making changes in his life before he turned fifty. All he wanted to do was learn how to dance (I am also a dance instructor). On his first lesson with me he was so nervous I could feel it through his entire body as I held his hands. He would frequent social dancing but would stand in the background, he felt socially awkward, he had no confidence and an abundance of fear for pretty much everything so much so he would go to the social dance late and leave early. He would stand and watch the couples on the dance floor just wishing that one day he would be half as good. He told me all he wanted to do was drive his car to the dance, have the ability not to consume alcohol enjoy dancing with ladies and then go home. That first night we sat chatting for hours about spirituality and general life happenings. He was intrigued about my life coaching and how it may help him become more confident. In the following weeks he spent one hour with me dancing and a separate hour for his coaching. He was so eager to learn, I was beginning to run out of ideas for new dance moves. As a farmer he would practice these moves whenever he had time and most of that time was while feeding his livestock dancing up and down the parlour remembering what he was taught. Mark achieved his only wish that he originally had, in fact he achieved much more. Six months after learning how to dance and having a belief in himself he is easily the first person out on the dance floor, he has an abundance of ladies wanting to dance with him and he was asked to dance in front of a television camera for a program to be aired early next year, he joyfully accepted the request no matter that others said to him 'people will laugh at you'. He had the best day recording the television program it was full of laughter and an experience that he was confident enough to allow into his life. Mark had no companionship when he first began socialising, so what he next asked for was wonderful friends, again his wish was granted he now has great company both male and female, this too came with learning on his journey to finding great friendship. He carried an abundance of fear one of those fears was asking a lady if she would like to dance. I am certain many can relate to the next part whether it is on a dance floor or in your life, that fear of rejection the little voice would go off inside his head 'you are not good enough' 'she will say no' 'you will look like a fool' 'who do you think you are' because his energy his vibration was fear based he could only attract people of that low vibration, he comfortably stayed in the presence of negative people even though he didn't like the words they would talk about others he knew at least he wouldn't have to stand by himself and he wouldn't have to risk asking someone for a dance because he would always receive it in this company. He was attracting people that did not have much self love for that is what he was unknowingly projecting out about himself, we can only attract to us the same energy back. As the weeks progressed through his coaching he learnt more on how to change his thoughts, he learnt how to love himself, he learnt how to let go of anger that lay within him towards others, he learnt how to be aware when fear was stepping in because it would most certainly come in on many different areas of his life. As his learning grew his vibration changed it was effortless for him to step away from the presence of others that were not on that same frequency. As effortless as it was for him for the others he stepped away from it was not the case there was a backlash and onslaught of nasty and degrading remarks, he never wanted to hurt anyone but he had to be mindful that these remarks he received were of no reflection on him he knew that was all the giver could offer him because that was all they had inside of them. It had been ten years from his last relationship the reason for the long period was healing time, it was a very painful time in Marks life and would take time to rebuild trust, belief and faith in himself and others. This new found excitement of dancing was amazing. Receiving attention was flattering until one day he said 'I am not feeling the excitement that I once did' I asked him 'do you believe you are ready for a relationship?' To which he replied 'yes I believe I am ready'

He had received all he had desired from his dancing to wonderful new friends now he was ready to receive a relationship. Part of the coaching was to write down exactly the type of lady he wanted. What he found attractive about her both inside and out. Did she enjoy dancing? What she smelt like? What were her hobbies? Was she financially sound? Did she have children? What does it feel like being in her presence? It was all up to mark and his imagination he had to believe this lady already existed in his life and feel every word he wrote as though she were sitting beside him. He was marvellous with this new homework, the imagination flowed I could feel her presence as I read the words he had written down. Mark continually worked with me changing the negative thoughts, releasing any frustrations and worries that he had. I wanted him to be on the highest frequency possible to attract the highest frequency lady into his life. When you are on a high frequency you are of love, joy, peace and enlightenment. Adding onto Marks coaching I began doing hands on energy work which was all about the heart space and opening it up. So many beautiful things took place through it, he was able to send love and light to those that were constantly in his pressured head, the cure for that pressure were daily headache tablets but after our first session he was able to set the tablets to one side the pressure had now been released. Mark told me that while walking into his home he could feel the lady walk in front of him with a cup of tea in her hand it was almost like he could see her. I told him it has already happened your timeline has not yet caught up with it. His next piece of homework was to go and purchase a toothbrush for this lady for she will require it when she comes to your home. He willing went to the store and purchased a pink toothbrush the most important part I want to state here is that Mark actually believed he was buying this for his new lady friend she had already manifested even though she had not yet made it to his presence it was an acting as if it had already happened. A few weeks later a lady that he often admired was at the social dance Mark found the courage to walk over and ask her for a dance, she told him she had seen him many times and often wished he would ask her to dance. The following day they both were at another venue in a different part of the country neither had arranged this. The friendship was formed each enjoying others company and from that dates followed. One day the lady was at his home and just as Mark predicted she walked in front of him with her cup of tea. Another evening as they were preparing to go out for the evening the lady turned to Mark and said "I would dearly love to brush my teeth after the food, would you have a spare toothbrush"?

However the toothbrush story does not end there. After several dates the little cracks began to show both parties were feeling the connection less as it turned out this was not the lady the toothbrush was destined for. I sat in my silence one evening confused as to why this had happened because Mark had carried out everything I had asked of him. That very same evening I received a phone call from Mark and it became evident as to why. "I need to tell you something Evelyn, the day I went to purchase a toothbrush instead of getting only one I purchased two". By this act alone he had sent all the mixed messages hurling out into the universe that I don't believe or perhaps I will get a second toothbrush just in case, don't put all your eggs in one basket. We are so conditioned throughout our lives for the 'just in case' or 'worst case scenario' we ask for one thing but then our actions and words bring forth our actual belief and the message we send out. I told him to immediately throw one toothbrush in the dustbin and get back on track to what he was putting out to the Universe. Sometime in the following few weeks Mark went on a date with a lady he had never met personally, it was arranged through a third party and from that another date then another both enjoying each other's company and the many meet ups. This time it felt different it was effortless everything developed in the perfect time. One evening while he visited the home of his lady friend she turned to him and said "I shall have to get you a toothbrush for my home" Mark silently laughed into himself, he said he will never look at a toothbrush the same way again.

They both continue to have a beautiful relationship which is blossoming into something very special.

The beauty in the story is that Mark only began with one wish as his journey progressed he became clearer on what he wanted to bring to his life. He took inspired action, he faced his many fears, he released and let go of anger and frustration in doing this he was able to receive the good this life has to offer. It is amazing what can happen in a short space of time. Be patient because if everything you wished for arrived all at the one time you would be so overwhelmed it would send you into fear and panic you would find it difficult to accept. If Mark knew that first night he came to me for a dance lesson what would manifest in the following months he would never have believed it therefore stopping the belief before it even had a chance to begin.

# *Allowing the flow*

*Stay low like the mighty ocean and allow all to flow
to you – Lao Tzu Ancient Chinese Philosopher*

I remember when I first read the above quote I placed the book on my lap and thought on it for quite some time. I had the vision of the mighty ocean and all of the rivers flowing into it, what a beautiful reflection of how our lives could be if we just mastered the art of allowing. If the ocean were to rise high it would stop every river from flowing to it and ultimately cease being the natural force that it is. Today as I write this chapter I reflected on particular happenings in my own life. I stood looking out of my bedroom window at a garage in my back yard, windows falling apart, no proper door, it was home to an old car and a place for fire wood to be chopped. I had very little money but as I stood looking out on that rainy day I could envision my dance studio being there. I could see so many people coming to me for lessons, I could see a new white car in my yard, I could hear laughter and I could feel the joy as people danced around my studio floor. I felt it all as though it were real. I had no idea how any of this would actually happen but I held onto that dream one day I will have it all. Today I do have my dance studio and the new white car, I have taught an abundance of people, I have heard their laughter and on this day as I write a television production company will film in my dance studio. None of this required force it came to me effortless. I walked to the section in the old garage where the fire wood was being chopped I was shocked when I saw the beginnings of a partition, my brother Gary was present I asked him what it was for he looked at me and said 'this is going to be your dance studio Nel' (a name that my father and brother fondly refer to me as – the origins of it is still unclear)

I want to thank you Gary, that thoughtful action you done for me on that day has helped change my life, I know there are many more I could thank you for I would have to write an entire book for all of those many thanks. Also stepping into my dance studio was a national newspaper for which I received a three page spread. On both occasions with the television company and newspaper I received random telephone calls, it all happened effortless. The reason I wanted to share this story with you is not for bragging purpose but rather as a reminder of Lao Tzu's quote 'stay low like the mighty ocean and allow all to flow to you'. When I organised my first retreat in the Canary Islands it all happened effortless I familiarised myself with the area, I choose the accommodation , learnt myself how to drive on the opposite side of the road, I went through the experiences myself and just asked who would like to attend, that is how a wonderful week was had by six ladies. Remember none of the experiences will make or break you they are what they are and that is simply an experience. You may have heard the saying 'never get above your station' even though it may not be the most encouraging of sayings I believe sometimes when people say it in a roundabout way it is to keep us grounded or maybe it could be delivered as a 'who do you think you are' so maybe in future rather than saying to someone who is progressing in their lives 'never get above your station' we could replace it with 'stay low like the mighty ocean and allow all to flow to you'. Whatever greatness happens to you throughout your life remember it is just another platform or opportunity for you to bring your joy and love to the lives of others we are all equal.

Next time you are by a river or stream stop and look at it and how it flows. There is no effort required, yes there are rocks and debris that may fall in its way but it still continues to flow, it runs free and so to shall you when you allow that effortless flow to enter your life.

We have said many times to friends and family 'just be yourself' we must allow them to be just that *themselves*. We ask this of people but then we also expect them to change for us to make our lives easier, we can be a complicated race sometimes, telling people one thing and then expecting something else. But just like the river and life we must allow the flow, we must allow people to be themselves and learn for themselves. If they are on the wrong path or not being true to themselves they will soon learn but that is not of our concern. Allow life to flow allow people to be themselves, allow your heart to guide you and you will come to know an effortless life.

# *If Only It Was That Easy*

After writing my first book 'A Life You Want' a step by step guide on how we manifest a life we want many people have said 'if only it was that easy'. It always brings a smile to my face when I hear these words. I am certain there is something you do in your life and perhaps someone has said to you 'you make that look easy/effortless'. I am in awe of people that produce beautiful food, it looks effortless but for some reason when I make an attempt it looks nowhere near how they produced it. Ice skaters, sports people, dancers, makeup artists, stylist, musicians how effortless they make everything look but we know that there must have been a lot of hours practiced, a lot of highs and lows to have it look so effortless. When it comes to our thoughts and because they belong to only us we believe that for certain this is one thing I can master, simple, right?

We have heard the motivational speakers, the gurus, the spiritual leaders and the man or woman you may randomly be speaking with say the words 'when you change your thinking you will change your life'. Perhaps if you have read my first book or similar books regarding law of attraction you had the thought that I once had, 'okay this seems straight forward, I don't really believe it can be that simple but sure let's give it a go'. So you make an attempt and nothing changes, what you wanted doesn't show up, but the great thing was it did work for you because even though your initial request was placed for what you wanted the actual feeling and subconscious thought was ' I don't really believe this'.

Changing your thoughts and beliefs are not simple when your first begin in fact it's a constant battle of 'what was I thinking'. It all begins with awareness, begin today to bring your awareness to the words you speak, instead of reacting with words that are not of love take a deep breath and change the delivery. It is not about judging others on what they are saying and how they are acting it all must begin with ME, MYSELF, YOURSELF. Just learn one thing at a time instead of the need to master everything all at once. Perhaps try this over the next few days and see how you get on.

*I AM Willing to teach myself how to become more aware of my words*

At the end of each day write down those words you said today that were not of support, compassion, love. 'I told you not to do that', 'you should have listened to me', maybe the person that drove their car out in front of you the words you uttered or yelled were just a reaction. Have you spoken poorly of someone today? Even though you believe you came from a place of love and you were right in what you spoke did it really help the other person or did it only make you feel better? Are you constantly complaining? The complainer doesn't know they are the problem they believe everything and everyone outside of them is wrong. When you have written or thought about your words today just bring awareness to how tomorrow you can bring change and come at conversations from another angle if you find this exercise difficult my advice is to say nothing and just listen. You only have control over your own thoughts and words, through time the awareness will be effortless. By changing how we deliver our words and the tone we use you will soon become aware that a situation and people change because you changed. By now we should have all passed the childish thinking of 'why should I be nice to her/him when she/he is not nice to me'

| *Child* | *Adult* |
| --- | --- |
| I hate you | I love you |
| I have to do everything | You do such a wonderful job |
| I hate this food | Look how strong you are |
| I'll never treat my kids like this | I will love your kids as much as I do you |

A lot of adults speak as the child does, just remember who you want to be when you respond.

Remember manifesting/creating/law of attraction never ceases to exist. It is happening this very second, what you want to show up in your life speak words as though it has. You must be a vibrational match for that which you wish to create in your life.

Be aware of the words you are speaking and saying to yourself negative self-talk is the worst self-harm you can bring to your mind, your body, your soul and your life. Some of the reasons why manifesting may not be working the way you thought it would

- Your words do not match up e.g. you may be thinking of a new job and visualising what you want but while speaking to others you may say words such as 'it so difficult to find work' 'I'm not good enough for what they want'

- Your belief does not match up. Are you going back to previous experiences in your life and holding onto that same belief you did at that time when things did not work out for you?

- You are wanting something from a place of fear. Are you looking for that wonderful relationship because you have a fear of being lonely? Are you wanting to look slimmer because you feel ugly? Remember, what you put your attention on will grow, lonely and ugly is what is taking place.

- Perhaps this was not for your highest good. I know when something does not show up in my life that something better much more than I could envisage is waiting for me.

What you put your attention to you will bring about into your life. Here is one example, a lady in her fifties was speaking with a few of us, she was telling us that her foot was giving her trouble and that she would have to get an insole fitted to help her arch. She said in all her life her feet never caused her any concern. A few days prior to the pain she sat in her car watching people going about their business on a busy Saturday in her local town. She was very focused on the abundance of people who were using walking aids like crutches, sticks and mobility scoters, she was amazed at the amount of people who required aid in order to walk. Sure enough a few days later her own foot began with the pain. When I said that she brought it about because of the attention she put on those who struggled with walking she rolled her eyes and said that's a lot of nonsense. This is how effortless it is to bring about things in our lives and even though she never wished this for herself what she transmitted through her thoughts and feelings it was created. 'Surely God knows we don't want these bad things in our lives', it is often been said. There is no good or bad with the universal energy/God/Divine it is what it is and you are the one who has free will to create what you want. When my youngest son shouted out Donald Trump has become the new president I wasn't surprised simply because of the sheer energy force he had received from everyone whether it was in favour or opposition he was still receiving the energy, from your thoughts and feelings. Next time you think 'If only it were that easy' think again because it only becomes easy when you bring full awareness to the words you speak, to what you put your attention on, to whom and what you surround yourself with, to what you read, watch on the television, the lyrics in music and the words you speak to yourself. Remember take the focus of what you do not want and place it on what you do want.

It becomes effortless for people to have constant drama in their lives. Work, children, money, health, partners, neighbours even going to the store can be a drama. Can you sit and ask yourself do I only thrive on drama? What are the stories I am constantly telling my friends? What am I posting on social media? I have come to know the most kindest people but with so much drama and they simply cannot seem to find a way out of it or perhaps don't want to find a way out of it 'who will I be without drama?'

Why do people create constant drama in their lives? Is it because a parent didn't show them attention when they were young? Did they have to do something major or become sick in order to receive attention? Are they always seeing the problem and never the solution? Do they believe they wouldn't be interesting to people without a dramatic story? You will constantly create more drama in your life with this behaviour and unfortunately you will find that the good people who stepped in to help you with your problems will soon step away in order to protect themselves if you are not willing to make change. So ask yourself am I the repellent who pushes people away? Or am I the light that draws all goodness to me?

# DECLAN – When the student is ready the teacher shall appear

With my Catholic up bringing I had always felt a connection to God which in my mind and in the teachings I was learnt through school and church was that God was the divine power a creator outside of me. Later in my life after going through many difficult situations and lessons as I began to open my mind, to read more and listened to many with alternative beliefs I came to realise that the power of this divine creator was within me, that I was part of that creation in fact I was the most magnificent part of creation.

While going through a not so pleasant time I searched for God to help me. The reason I went in search was that I wanted God to help me stay in my marriage. I had made a promise to God on the day I got married to be with my husband until death do us part. I felt such sadness I felt guilt and all I wanted was for God to help me keep this promise I made. I read parts of the bible for answers for a solution to my yearning. I visited many different dominations church services. I remember it was Easter and a pastor asked if anyone was ready to be saved. As a newbie to this church just on a flying visit to find God I felt as if a spotlight was beaming onto me. I have yet to experience the menopause but what I felt at that time I can only imagine resembled ten hot flashes. I could feel the sweat trickle down my spine. I began to slide down on the chair praying that he wouldn't look at me. It's funny thinking back to it now, my thoughts were 'Oh sweet Lord how the hell will I go back to my catholic home and say I've been saved surely my life would have to change'. Many thoughts danced in my mind 'I'll have to send my children to a different school' 'I'll have to stop cursing and taking any alcohol, my family will totally disown me' yip I just wanted the ground to open up and swallow me. Thankfully he moved on to another conversation but that soon softened my cough I never set foot back through the door of that church again, I would just have to find God somewhere else. Breaking my promise to God was the most difficult challenge I had to face. I met with my parish priest months later after I had left my marriage, I told him of the guilt I still carried breaking the promise. He was the priest who had married me and christened two of my children. He had no judgement on me in fact as we stood by the bread section in the local store he said that his door was always open if I ever wanted to call and have a chat with him. He has since passed but I did enjoy every random encounter we had. He was a business man, I'm not sure if he would have had much in common with the 'ordinary folk' but I always enjoyed our chats, I would tell him how handsome he was looking and have a laugh. I hope it was refreshing for him that for a few minutes someone didn't notice the collar he wore and treated him as they would any other person.

Fast forward a few years later by this time I had began opening my mind to much more than my constricted beliefs around God. I had heard of a man by the name of Declan Coyle but never felt an urge to go see him, with the exception of this one time, a time that would inevitable change my life and bring me the answer I was searching relentlessly for. Firstly when this man began to speak something came into my head 'Evelyn you are going to speak alongside this man one day' at this time I was not doing any public speaking. I certainly did not have the confidence and something still felt incomplete within me. It was a two day event I knew most of what he spoke about, I sat patiently waiting on that bomb shell because again that voice came in or the thought 'there is a reason why you are here'. As the second day was coming to a close I so yearned to hear something from this wonderful man and then it came in his closing words. He said 'let's talk about God', I almost leapt out of my skin with sheer excitement, my entire inside was going off like a fireworks display but the outer shell remained still and calm. I felt like a priory dog twitching its head from side to side 'was there anyone else in this room feeling the excitement'?

He began 'The God that you know as the man in the clouds with the beard and staff is as real as the tooth fairy'. I find it difficult to describe how I felt with those words, this man who may I add was a Catholic priest for many years a man who served the Catholic Church and its teachings a man who knew his bible inside out was now delivering this message with no fear, no anger, no resentment, only pure love such a taboo topic that we dare not speak about. This man had just opened a whole new can of worms no one dare speak of God like this or so I was brought up to believe.

The final words he said will forever be ingrained in my mind, my heart and my soul. Words that no one had ever told me my entire life, when he said the words a rush of breath filled my lungs like it was the first breath I had ever taken in my entire life. I could breath, I felt life in me, I remembered who I was.

## *'YOU ARE A HOST TO GOD'*

Even though I had never heard these words before I just knew in every part of my being 'there you have it Evelyn you were the answer all along'. In my search to find God and asking that he help me stay in my marriage I realised I was asking the wrong question. All I needed to ask was guide me to my peace and that was the day I found my peace because I had found God within me.

Declan and I did share a stage together, he was the guest speaker at my first book launch, he wrote the foreword to my book 'A Life You Want' and it all happened effortless.

We don't need to know how things are going to happen in our lives, we must master the art of patience, allowing and just let events unfold in their own time when the great universal energy knows we are ready. I want to say a massive thank you to Declan Coyle – Author of The Green platform, he has been and continues to be a wonderful teacher and mentor to me. I have learnt so much from the first day we met and above all else we have become great friends.

To the reader of this book inside you right at this present time there are many talents and abilities ready to surface. So much has happened in my life from meeting Declan. Be thankful for all of the great teachers in your life, they all come to us in very different ways. For the father that did not show you love, he has taught you how to be a more loving person. For the friend or work colleague who is always annoying you, they are your teacher for patience. For the child who rebels against what you tell them they are your teacher of trust and releasing of control. With this new found freedom I felt from the unveiling that I was a host to God I began to experience my life very different knowing and feeling I was off and part of this Divine energy. Let's experience one day from that Spirit, open your eyes to see everything and everyone as this divine energy. I had a clear understanding that in order for me to see with my human senses everything around me had to form/manifest into something of form.  I imagined that if an enormous eraser came out of the sky wiping everything out it would still remain as the divine energy the only difference would be that as a human I would not be able to see the form it would all be one massive ball of energy and to me that realisation made perfect sense. We place names on everything that is formed from the divine energy and that is off the divine energy, names such as trees, houses , flowers, cars, humans, grass, water, earth, money, it's all energy it has just taken different form in order for us humans to see. *Uni-verse One song.* Everything is connected.

## *Children are our teachers*

From our children are born all we want for them is to be safe and to have a great life. We want to send them into education to obtain the best results possible to then go on and have a great job. When I was going through primary and secondary education I didn't give my parents much concern, I would get up early, dress myself and head of for the day to learn and enjoy. When it came my turn to be a parent my first child Erinrose had the same outlook as I did, I never had to ask her to get up in the morning or to do homework and I never received one phone call from the school with regards to her behaviour it was effortless to her and for me as a parent. Following on from that my two sons I really believe the Universe/God/Source had a different plan for them and for me regarding 'education'. The boys were very different when they entered their teenage years something changed they could not abide by the system that was in place for education or perhaps it was the ruler who governed over them in the education system, this very special position of authority had also changed hands from my daughters period in school. The rules, the instructions, the punishment and they questioned many times why they needed to learn information they would never use the rest of their lives. They wanted to ask questions especially on religion, questions that were not appreciated by the authority. They believed they could speak to their teachers the way they speak to their friends and the openness of conversations they would have at home, but again this was not tolerated perhaps because of legislation which was in place for the protection of the children and the teachers. One of my sons was and still is a bit of a comedian and being a teenage boy when he saw the word 'breast' on an exam paper to him this was an opening to permit his inner comedian out regardless of the back lash and the summoning of myself to yet another meeting at the school. For my son his teenage remark on the exam paper had done even better than he had intended because now the teachers and myself had also heard it, to him it was like a video on YouTube that had just gone viral. I have had many lessons, learnings and more importantly I as a parent have grew from these past three years of learning. There have been many suspensions, detentions and meetings.

With my first boy I had been beckoned to the school so many times that while on a journey to my work I received the final phone call I was willing to receive. I could hear in my mind

*'If nothing changes, nothing changes. If you keep doing what you are doing you are going to keep getting the same results. You want change? Then make it.'*

I done something that day to many would seem crazy and as many said to me 'why'?

I told the principal I was removing my son from school the reason for this my son was not happy, the principal was not happy and I was not happy. The same things would have continued to happen over and over. My son would have done something not to the satisfaction of the school, I would receive a phone call and either suspension, detention or a meeting would follow. Time and time again this would happen, I made the choice that NOW was the time for change otherwise nothing would have changed. In your life are the same patterns happening over and over? Are you waiting on someone or some situation to change before you decide to make the change? Of course change does not come without fear, fear of the unknown. Questioning yourself on the decision you will make, worrying what others will think, stressing over the impact it will have on others. My main duty of responsibility was for my son and I am blessed that my thinking had changed so much in all of my years of finding my God within. The words flowed effortless from me because I know and I believe that as long as you have a dream or a knowing what you bring your joy to and what brings you joy, that talent, ability that lies within you which you bring forth to help mankind you will always get their because this is your purpose in life. I do not believe the more qualifications you possess the more joyful you will live your life. We as humans have placed such a huge emphasis on qualifications and yes it opens up opportunities if the academic route is your passion and joy. When you find your love and peace in creating from your heart, rules, orders, being the same as everyone else, wearing the same uniform (even the word uni-form one-form the form is all exterior we have many different forms), learning the same subjects will not necessarily work. A lot of parents love to tell others how well their children are performing at school, what university they will attend, what grades they have obtained, how intelligent their child is and this is okay but many times it is because it's all a reflection on the parent and how well they have brought their children up and perhaps as the parent you did not achieve all you wanted so your child's academic results layers over the disappointment you have felt with what you believe were missed opportunities or 'I could have done much better in life if I had achieved better examination results'. We have pride we love that people speak well of our children and of course we want to show our praise and pride to others.

That day I drove to the school and removed my son from the education system. I remember the departing words his principal said to my son ' I am disappointed in you'. I never replied but I do know this you can have all the education in this world and never realise the impact that one sentence will have on a young mind.

I am grateful that we have so many wonderful people in our education system that can relate to young people. I am grateful that these educators awaken every morning full of joy and love for what they do and what they will deliver that day. I am so very grateful that there are many people in the education system who can separate the issue from the child they can see that the child is not 'bad' that they see the child just needs education on how best to deal with their emotions and express themselves without fear of punishment but to reward for the wonderful effort they are making to bring about change in their lives. I am grateful we have the great facilities to offer wonderful life lessons. I do pray and see a future that the old Industrial Age education system will change.

**Education** *'Educatum'* composed of two terms 'E' and 'Duco'

'E' implies a movement from inward to out and 'Duco' means developing or progressing. To nourish the good qualities in man and draw out the best in every individual.

Questions I ask myself as a parent am I drawing out the good qualities in my children, the love the joy and the dreams or am I more focused on their 'bad' behaviour, their inability to be like other children, their colourful words that they choose through anger and their actions they carry out with their changing hormonal teenage body. Have I expectations on what they should achieve through my visions, my dreams my outcomes? Does my child need to behave in a certain manner in order for me to show them love? Does my child need to achieve certain grades in order for me to tell them how proud I am of them? Does my child need to conform to systems and rules in order for me to approve of them?

What I have learnt is that my children are here as individuals to experience their own journey. They must learn what feels great and not so great from what they say, do , think and feel. I can only guide them by what I say and not force upon them. When you think back if someone was to tell you 'you must do what I tell you' there is a great chance you would do the opposite. I believe as adults we confuse fear and respect. If they fear me they will show me respect. So in order for them to fear me there will be consequences, there will be backlash. We dare not have spoke against our parents, our teachers, our clergy because if we did we knew what the punishment would have been so rather than respecting our peers we live in fear of them and quite possibly have a lot of deep seeded anger within us. I have learnt to let go of control, I have brought peace within myself and must be accepting of whatever comes my children's way. This is their journey if I was to shout constantly at them because of all their wrong doings all that I am teaching them is anger. I as a parent need to be able to show my children how to communicate to others without rage, something that is taking a bit of time for them to understand but it will all come in its right time. All we want for our children is to be happy in life, to respect themselves and others and have a positive mindset to be able to deal better in situations they once rebelled against. When is your child most happiest? What is the inner treasure your child holds that will bring a light to this world and the people of it?

I have learnt that children are our teachers. Watch the very young how great their imaginations are, how caring and loving they are and how they make you feel when they wrap their little arms around you. As they grow they change and we are moulding their beliefs and their thoughts by what we are showing them. What they have been watching on television, what they watch on social media, what gaming they are hooked on. Your child will succeed in this life as long as they know they have your love, as long as they know they have all the magnificence within them to bring their dreams to life. Depending on what your version of success is but for me and what I teach my children is to bring joy to your life and the lives to others. No one makes you angry you make that choice yourself of which my children remind me when they detect a change of tone in my voice. Let them dream their dream, it does not matter what qualifications they have by the laws of the universe it will all be delivered to them it is not your or their concern to work out the 'how' part. Patience, compassion, releasing control and acceptance are the many lessons I have learnt the very reasons I was chosen to be the mother of two boys that did not conform to the system. I continue to learn and grow as they do through these many lessons in our daily lives together. One day they will be parents of teenagers, I have a smile on my face with that vision I have an inkling granny may be called upon when their teenagers begin the cycle all over again. I will watch what my children have learnt and how they transmit that to their children. Give blessings for your children, they don't understand what it is like to be an adult they are stuck in that place of neither child or adult and it's confusing for them so perhaps it's up to us adults to understand and remember what it was once like to be a child. I wish to express my utmost gratitude to Declan Coyle for my understanding of education through his loving, compassionate and knowledgeable delivery on the subject.

# Being at Peace

B eing at peace almost sound like a destination. I am at work, I am at my friends, I am at home, I am at the supermarket, to say I am at peace feels like a location where I am but not who I am.

*I AM PEACE*

So how do we bring ourselves to that peace? How do we become peace? You are from peace, you are peace within so therefore you can only be that of peace.

R.I.P *rest in peace,* our mind does not think of peace, we feel a darkness, a sadness and death. What if we had L.I.P *live in peace* or P.I.L *peace in living.* Why must we wait until the body dies before we bestow wishes of restful peace. Can you bestow upon yourself that today I shall live in peace and I will know peace in living? The spirit is infinite it shall you shall return onto that energy of weightlessness and peace it is only on this earthly plain that humans have forgotten what they are from spending a life time searching for that from once they came. I believe that is why we are discontent with what we have, I believe it is why we want to keep achieving more material gatherings and wealth into our lives. I believe it is why we turn to food, alcohol, drugs, relationships any kind of addiction because it's a searching of a fulfilment that we yearn for. We have always known but somehow forgotten, we are trying to recreate or find that thing that is inside us, that feeling. Buried deep in your discontentment, your under achievement, your unworthiness, your guilt, your doubt, your fear, your righteousness, is a glint of the most precious creation it looks like an object glistening in a distance that which the sun reflects upon on a beautiful summers day. You will find what you have been searching for and even though you don't believe you are searching, until you find that precious peace within only then will you realise you had been a treasure hunter most of your life, but now you have found your Aladdin's cave.

The beauty with being peace is that everything becomes effortless, you can certainly wish for many things to manifest into your life but with inner peace you have a non attachment to the outcome you will permit the outcome to form itself. When you are at peace you surrender to the higher power to the divine energy to the will of God this does not mean you give up on yourself or life, but with surrender it is letting go of having to control all outcomes. Surrender is what makes you powerful. If you have peace within you right now no matter what comes your way should that be all the riches in the world or a crisis you will be at peace, in peace and be peace. Can you picture yourself just observing others and events happening around you and feeling that peace knowing everything is as it should be, seeing the solution rather than the problem and understanding the only thing you need to do is follow your heart, speak your truth from your heart, bring joy to your life and the lives of others. At the end of a mass service the final words from when I was last there were 'Go in peace and serve the Lord' *Go be peace and follow your heart.* You have a purpose here you will find it in your peace.

## *Sense of Entitlement*

After an insightful conversation with a friend this morning I felt inspired to put pen to paper and write on something that I believe is effecting a lot of families, individuals and society. At some time in your life you have said or heard it said 'he/she believes they are entitled to …..' Stop for a moment think back to your childhood and how your parents brought you up. My father's generation had very little of anything. Their fathers were the workers the providers and the mothers were the care takers working tirelessly hand washing clothes, growing crops, seeing to the children there was no sense of entitlement. What food you were given you appreciated, what clothes you had you took care of and what you earned you worked hard for and all from a very young age. My generation growing up when I look back there were lots of times when money would not have been plentiful, second hand clothes were always welcomed and we looked forward to our parents pay day for the treats and little luxuries. I don't recollect anyone driving fancy cars and if you were going out to the discotheque if your parents had the money to hand over you would have enough to pay your admission and purchase a drink. But as the years progressed things began to get a little better. Follow onto today's generation which I believe has seen a massive jump with technology, money, cars, houses etc and perhaps some may think a sense of entitlement.

A man my generation began with very humble beginnings, through the years he started up a business which has grew from strength to strength he is now a millionaire. The youngest of his two sons came to work for him it had been his first and only job. The son comes to work late, doesn't partake in any meetings, has a wonderful apartment in a city location and a great car. The father is under serious duress and is becoming increasingly frustrated with the son and his sense of entitlement that he is taking the company, his income and his high standard of living for granted. There is many a parent that feels the strain of demands put onto them by their children and feeling that they need to keep up to date with all the modern ways of the world. We feel this generation have a sense of entitlement but actually they don't  they probably don't even know what that means. They just know what they have learnt and that is if I ask often enough there is a good chance I'll get what I want. What we as parents have done is rob our children of those experiences we had growing up. We have tried to protect them from the embarrassment, the shame, the worry of not having money so we have continuously gave them possessions, holidays, money, latest name brand clothing to prevent them from experiencing some of those not so pleasant feelings we had as children. If you think back to when you were younger on that one day you got the treat, you got the new shoes, you got the day trip away, can you remember the total gratitude and joy you felt? I have said to my children as my mother had said to me 'you are so ungrateful', lack of appreciation but unknowingly we just expected it, not for one second did I realise how hard my mother or father worked to give me it and the same for my own children. I remember my mother and father taking us on our first major holiday to America, when I think back now my attitude makes me feel unwell. I was seventeen, I came in late from a night out without a care for anyone else except myself. Our flight was departing in eight hours, I only started packing my suitcase. I remember my mother getting very angry with this laid back attitude I had easily adopted how I did not appreciate what herself and my father were doing for us, I looked at her and said "I never asked to go in the first place" those words must have really hurt my mother. A holiday that she was so excited to take us on, a trip she dieted for months before hand, a trip that cost a fortune and here I was not one ounce of excitement, no consideration for anyone else's feelings except my own. I actually was more exited the first time mum took us all in the VW beetle to the swimming pool. The car packed to capacity not a seat belt of any kind required and us bouncing around the back seat like wound up toys, oh how I am sure she wished I had been a bit more like that in my teenage years. The title effortless is what a lot of younger people feel rather than sense of entitlement Ask and you shall receive. As parents we want to keep our children safe and protected but we have a duty of care to equip them with all of the tools they need to manage their mental wellbeing and emotions. When the child is learning to walk we let go of their hand and allow them to take those first steps by themselves, if they fall we pick them up and gradually through time if they fall they know how to pick themselves up. If we were never to let go constantly walking around with them on our hip of course they would begin to weigh us down and we would become frustrated that they can't walk but if you don't permit them the experiences of falling and rising, of feeling the pain from the fall that enviably passes they will never learn they will never experience the beauty of running on a beach, of climbing hills, they will never truly experience gratitude. We take our fresh air for granted because we have always had it, let us respect it rather than poison it because I for one definitely do not want to be without it. Permit your children to learn from all of their lessons, for one day you will not be there to protect them and how then will they manage the lows in their lives if we have always been their safe guard. I am of the belief we have no entitlements in this life instead we have something more precious the privilege of experiencing this glorious creation for one more day. There is a beautiful generation growing up, a generation that will bring light to this world.

# *The cross over*

With anything I write I want to keep it in simplistic form for readers who may have questions on how we create an effortless life. I have titled this chapter *'the cross over'* for me that's exactly what it was, the cross over from the God I had been brought up with to the scientific beliefs. I was terrified at the thought of 'what if all I had believed in all of my life doesn't exist?' the thought alone had me questioning why I even wanted to go snooping around in this quantum physic world.

*Be brave Evelyn open your mind a little and go exploring.*

I tend to see life as one big department store with everyone who is here to help mankind having their own little store within. I thought I'll open the quantum physic store door just a little bit and have a look inside. They say curiosity killed the cat but I knew I wasn't going to die it was the curiosity and an urge to find out more of what was 'out there' that egged me on. My first discovery was a man by the name of Gregg Braden he spoke about the lost gospels of Thomas. So many discoveries have been made throughout the years of gospels that have mysteriously been omitted from the bible. In the lost gospels Thomas wrote

*when you make the two, thought and emotion one you will say to the mountain move away and it will move away.*

When the two become one in our heart we create the feeling. The feeling is the prayer, feel as if your prayers are answered.

*If the two make peace with each other in this house they will say to the mountain move away and it will move away (you are the house)*

*Ask and you shall receive* we must communicate what the quantum field recognises and this is not with our voice but combining your very thought and the emotion. The field recognises the magnetic waves our heart produces. When you create the feeling in your heart as if the prayer is already answered that is what creates the electrical and magnetic waves that bring the answer to you.

My wish for you after reading this is to be clearer that in fact the science and spiritual world are pretty much all the same they are just delivered differently. It is the one divine energy, source that is nameless but that which we choose to name as God, Universe, Divine, Source, Allah, Buddha, Quantum field, Energy. One day I cried profusely asking why people thanked the universe and not God? I could never ask God for anything but I had no problem asking the Universe, ohh how our teachings have misguided us but perhaps we were just taught what their limited minds only knew. People who do not believe the church teachings of God are very much swayed in the direction of the quantum physic world and the many laws of the Universe. When you begin to open your mind, learn, read and watch people you will begin to notice that when you change the way you see things the things you see will inevitably change. When I speak to people I will use different terminology depending what feels more comfortable with the person, it is all the same. When we use the word God or think of the word as a man do you see someone who will judge you? Punish you? Be angry with you? Do you see your God as someone you get angry with for the difficult periods in your life? Do you blame your God for the catastrophes and starvation in this world? Your God is the divine source energy of infinite love from which you have came and from what you are of and that which you are a host to, even if it's the Big Bang theory you are still of it and what an entrance to make with a Big Bang. The God energy is within everything it is the seen and unseen we have portrayed God as a man because this is the form taken in order for humans to relate and to know you are of the same. As a child and young adult when I heard of the holy trinity the father, the son, and the Holy Spirit that it was one I was very confused. How can one person be three? Of course it's possible because it is all the one divine energy source we were just looking at it through a human mind and eyes. The I AM is everything. The bible is littered with I AM's this is how God is referred to. My personal take on the commandment 'Thou shalt not take thy Lord thy God's name in vein' I truly believe thy Lord thy Gods name is I AM so whenever you choose to speak the words I AM you are speaking about that which you are of. Should you choose to follow it with a word or words that do not serve you that is when you are taking thy Lord thy Gods name in vein. I am ugly, I am poor, I am ill, I am unworthy, I am not deserving, I am stupid, I am disgusting, I am guilty, I am useless think carefully what you follow your I AM with today because as you say sayeth so shall it be. I am wonderful, I am beautiful, I am gifted, I am love, I am grateful, I am financially abundant, I am ready for an amazing life, I am blessed.

I have asked people who practice law of attraction if they see God and the Universe as separate the answer is normally yes. I for one also saw them as separate when I first began. My understanding was that the universe was always giving and I could easily receive I never saw the universe as a human form just one massive eternal abundant universe giving me what I was transmitting through my thoughts feelings and actions. God on the other hand was a man that I said thank you to and be happy with what I have, I never would have dreamt of asking God to provide me with wonderful experiences in this life. You may see the Universe as the planetary system but the reference to the Universe is the infinite source energy, all giving & all loving. When you have a thought and the feeling of gratitude of it already happening you release, you transmit that from you in the form of energy into the universe energy, the quantum field, it will attract to the same energy and draw it back to you. Even if you are feeling unwell if you affirm that I am healthy, I am growing stronger, I am well. If you can see that and try to feel yourself return to your wellness, if you give gratitude for the wonders your body is, let that be the energy you release from you in order for your wellness to return. Should you choose to keep your focus on your illness, talking about it, complaining about your body you will continue to endure it or even worse for a longer period. You have free will on this earth, you are creating your life whether you decide to call your greater source God, Universe, Buddha, Allah, Tao, Mary, David it makes no difference it is whatever feels best for you and how best you feel your connection to source energy. God takes no offence to the name you choose, the Divine is nameless, it is only us humans that find offence. You are a host to the God Divine Energy, the Universal Energy, your Spirit, your inner light its whatever you choose to call it. It does take a lot of practice to become consciously aware of what thoughts we are omitting and the words we are speaking. Sometimes we automatically react to situations without thinking and not for the best outcome , perhaps each day try to become more aware. You will begin to notice peoples words especially if they are veering on the negativity side, again your automatic response maybe to jump in and say 'no don't be using those words' but just let it go, you only have to become aware without the judgement on either yourself or others. Feed your mind everyday with beautiful thoughts and gratitude for all you have and for all that you are. Take a look at yourself each morning in the mirror and begin to start speaking wonderful words to the reflection looking back at you. Have a dream, everything and anything is possible, if you have a vision and a calling or heart connection to do something, to move somewhere to learn something to phone someone don't stop the dream because you have no idea how it will all happen. The how is not your concern. I heard someone say 'well surely I have to do something'? The answer is yes what you must do is feel that it has already happened continue each day to do what makes you feel love and joy and depending on your dream if it is a home for example go visit it drive by it, get yourself a scrap book put images of items you would like for the home, see yourself being there. What does it feel like? Start putting what you can afford away, love and appreciate where you at living presently and let go of the outcome. If this is for your highest good all will be delivered. One of the most difficult parts for people including myself can sometimes be patience. Quantum physics deals with the tiniest particles of energy and all depending on our mood, feeling, emotion we transmit this energy on vibrations, for example guilt, fear, anger, anxiety would operate on a lower vibration whereas joy, love, peace and enlightenment are on higher vibrations ideally that is where you want to be and yes it can be difficult to stay on the high vibes all of the time but just bring awareness to your thoughts and your mood, if you are on a lower vibration try and change that thought, watch a movie that makes you laugh, play a game with your children, look at old photographs that bring a smile to your face and make you feel good, listen to some upbeat music, go for a walk or do some exercise. This doesn't mean to ignore your feelings it is perfectly okay to cry to feel sad these are very natural we must experience the feeling and emotions of loss, the tears we cry are unspoken words and healing for our soul. Energy travels in frequencies, our vibration goes to that frequency and draws back the same to us. If you have ever woke in the morning dreading the day ahead then one thing happens that makes you feel angry perhaps you slept in then there is a traffic jam your day just continues with one thing after another going every way but the right way you just wish for the day to be over, unfortunately you created the entire day yourself by how you began it. People find it difficult to believe they are the creators we are such powerful manifesting beings so if you can create a day that is not so good for you how about changing it around. Begin your morning with a thank you, be grateful for a new beginning to the rest of your life, declare that this day wonderful things will happen to me and through me. Get that feeling of joy what today will bring, notice the trees on your commute to work, listen to uplifting music, feed your mind with anything but the news first thing in the morning. Should you meet anyone that day who is not in a good mood just smile raise them to your vibration rather than you dropping to theirs. Spirituality and quantum physics are the same just different words and the physics part will always have evidence of how energy works with spirituality for me it's more a sense of feeling, belief, knowing and I see evidence of it all the time in my own life and the people I work with. I know that the Divine energy we have within is in all things seen and unseen, quantum physics will prove that for those who may need to be shown before they believe. We are a world and universe full of vibrating energy whatever your belief the end result is that you are creating your life, you have free will we are all from the one source which we will return to. It is only the manifested form which is our bodies that will die energy does not die your spirit does not die you are infinite. So make the journey in this life time the best you can. Live your dreams, love yourself, make changes, open your mind, let go of worries and fears the Divine energy will work out how all will come to you just live a life of joy or at least be willing.

*Today I am willing to embrace life. I am willing to love myself more. I am willing ...........(you finish this with what you feel)*

*With the discovery of quantum physics showing that everything is energy in various levels of vibration, it has now brought science & spirituality together to show that they are actually one & same thing. With this knowing, it can take our belief in co-creation of our life to a whole new level of fact. With aligning our thoughts of what we want, with a true feeling in our heart as if we already have it, we change our vibrational energy field & in doing so attract our desire to us from the quantum energy field of infinite possibilities!*

Mark A. McCloskey
Successmindset Life

# Change the way you see things

Q: If I am on a journey to keep myself in a positive mindset but others around me are being negative how do I change this?

A: You are only in control of your own thoughts, words and actions. You must learn to release control on anything outside of you. If someone is angry with you and they have made a choice not to speak with you, speak poorly about you or voice their anger towards you all you need to know is that they have stepped away from their true authenticity of divine love. When you see that person differently the situation will change. Whatever someone has filled themselves with that is all they can offer you. If I have only anger in me from events that have happened or I have unresolved issues lying dormant in my subconscious that I have not healed from, if I feel my parents didn't show me love, if I cannot accept myself , if I am jealous of others, if I feel empowered by putting others down that's my insecurities the list is endless but this is all I can offer you. It is not you I am angry with it is something within me I am angry with. If you are the person who is on the receiving end of anger either remove yourself from the situation or wait until the person has completely exhausted themselves of their words before you offer a solution to the problem. Do not react in the heat of the moment because in doing so this is your ego screaming at you 'how dare you speak to me like this' 'give as good as you get' 'show them you are right' 'hurt them even worse with your words' 'shout louder'. Nothing will ever be resolved. If you permit someone's words to filter in and you believe them this is when your self esteem will drop your confidence will hide in the shadows and your self love becomes almost extinct. What happens you spend days, months, years reading self help books, taking classes on self esteem and confidence, in order to try to love yourself again. Family members when angry can certainly say words that pierce your heart they know you better than anyone else, they know your weakness that is where they will inflict the most pain. Learning to have self control does take a lot of practice and it's something I work on every day. I cannot judge anyone else and then complain if someone judges me. When people behave in such a manner they are hurt and have forgotten the true beauty and love from which they have originated. I wish for them only peace and love in their hearts so they can get to experience a taste or glimpse of that beautiful feeling. For the person who chooses to speak the words not of love , let go of having to control. The mouth opens words stream out with no thought except to prove you are right and to tell the other person you have really upset me you have made me angry and this is the only way I know how to express myself. When people are angry I see them as actually voicing ' I have completely lost control I have given my power to you with this emotion surging through my body and these damaging words I choose to speak. I have a lot of self loathing within me from what others have said to me in the past, from what others have done on me. I am unaware that these words I scream at you are from a place within me. I am frustrated with my life, with myself , with everything and I do not know how to express myself other than what I am doing now because this is all I have learnt. I know no different, please forgive me, I hope I remember the love that I know is within me. Do not react to my actions and my words this is nothing you have done, it simply has triggered something with me that I need to heal, please show me compassion and love. I thank you for seeing who I really am'.

Remember you have free will if you are subject to verbal vulgarity or physical abuse respect and love yourself enough that if the other person is unable to make changes in their life and within themselves you are the only one who can control what you choose to do. Follow your heart, you are not to blame for someone else's rage. You are the only one that is in control of your thoughts, your words and your actions, always keep your power, protect your energy, choose not to be the victim but rather the victor of your precious life.

# *Honour your truth*

Have you questioned what is my purpose in this life? Why am I here? Have you a feeling within you that there is much more to this life? Have you a feeling that there is something much bigger at play? I can share with you what I feel, what I believe to be our truth. You can read, you can question and you can analysis and if after reading this chapter you feel something in your heart rather than your head there is something stirring within you. Your heart will guide you to your truth and it will come into battle with your head on more than one occasion, fear will step in, doubts creep in but know this is all part of the process, this happens to everyone even the person you most admire as being courageous, confident, intelligent they and I have had our fair share of doubt and fear, it will always find a way in but its noticing it and being brave enough to continue on your journey. Please allow your heart to guide you no matter what battles you may face. By choosing this path it will be the most rewarding for you and everyone else. You will receive joy, inner peace and that feeling of unconditional love, you will receive abundance in more ways than your human mind can comprehend. There is a chance I could be repeating on what I continually say but know that you are part of the greatest source of unconditional love, you have this within you. When we come to a time in our life that we truly know this, I honestly believe that this is when everything becomes effortless. I have countless friends that have had the courage to step away from situations which did not feel right, jobs that they no longer felt joy in delivering, relationships that had run its course. They had no idea what was next for them where the next job would come from where money would come from but they were prepared to have trust and faith that by following their hearts and battling through the mind thoughts that all would come to them. We all have a purpose in life and it is to bring joy to our lives and to the lives of others by not following the heart and by disconnecting your heart from its source it's impossible to live a life of fulfilment, we simply exist, we make do and for some this is perfectly okay. When they chose to step away from that which no longer served them this included the old negativity they constantly spoke to themselves bit by bit opportunities came to them, wonderful happenings came in order for them to live their purpose and bring joy to many. When opportunities come to us our belief grows stronger, by releasing old patterns, anger, frustration with things and people outside of us we open a gateway to allow all the beauty and magnificence this life can offer. The more the belief grows the more will come to you. You will come to an understanding that all of these experiences are just that 'experiences' it will not change who you are if you believe when you are earning lots more  money, have a grander title, live in a bigger home or socialise with the celebrities you are above others unfortunately your ego has now stepped in and you have disconnected from your heart and purpose. What is your dream? What is your calling? What has been coming to you time and time again that you wish you had the courage to do? Maybe when you think of that dream you get a beautiful feeling but then the blocks come up, I can't do this because I don't have the money, I would need to have money in place or my new job secured before I would contemplate taking action towards my dream. We have a need to control everything, we need to know the exact steps we have to take in order for something to happen in our lives. We go so far ahead of ourselves, thoughts that take us into the future the fear attached to that makes us lose sight of the present. I spoke with a lady who had been writing a book for ten years but that's as far as it went. When I told her publishing my book was done with ease she was amazed. Other people told her how difficult it would be and the  massive security of money she would need. I said if you want to write a book just write it the rest is effortless, don't listen to the horror stories especially when it's your dream and not theirs. Fears all seem perfectly normal because this was our human upbringing. Be safe, be careful, don't get ahead of yourself, it may not work out, what will people say? Remember what happened the last time, you can't do it, this isn't for you. Ah yes the human conditioning, living in a constant state of fear. The need to control, this is also fear.

Do what you can do, have an idea what the end result will look like, just sit and feel what it would be like when that happens, give gratitude for it being delivered. Be patient with yourself and the Universe when we start on anything we have a burst of motivation and then usually after a few weeks that slowly disappears. Motivation will not keep you going it will be your belief and trust. You do not need to concern yourself with how things will happen just begin and affirm

- *I am grateful for this day*

- *I am grateful for my passion*

- *I believe and trust that the right people will come my way at the right time for my dream to manifest*

- *Everything comes to me at an affordable price*

- *I am safe*

Just let go of having to control each step and the outcome do what your heart is guiding you to do. Be mindful who you share your dreams with, not everyone will think and feel as you do. It is wonderful to have support along your journey, I am blessed to have amazing people in my life, we live each other's dreams before they manifest into our present. You have free will, you choose and do what feels right for you, remember you are here to experience all that life has to offer. You are here to grow and help others with the joy and the learning you have gained from all of your experiences. Always speak with love, send love to situations and people that may not be to your pleasing. You are from the Divine eternal source energy, it is within you. Continue to remember your true authenticity. Honour the divine being that you are, honour your gifts and talents, honour every day you get to live this life.

# *Reconnect*

How do we create an effortless life? I listened to Morgan Freeman the actor say when he was a boy of five years old standing on a stage the words flowed effortless, he knew at that point what his calling in this life was. The odds were very much against him and no one could have foreseen the amazing joy this man would bring to our screens but he knew at age five why he was here. It's a feeling. It's a knowing. It's effortless.

Before I stand up to speak in front of audiences, before I settle down to write my book, before I meet with clients and before I begin my day, I sit in my silence and ask that all that be of me be of spirit. I know spirit will find the way through nervousness, doubt, fear. "May my words flow effortless from my mouth or through my pen" I just breathe. I listen to my heart rather than my egotistical thinking always the words will flow. It is almost that I am in a trance but still present or as people would say 'they were in the zone'. You are alive, you know why you are here, it is effortless to you because that is who you are. We must reconnect to our source of life, light and love for when we disconnect life becomes difficult, we have stepped away from that one divine energy that has only love for us, that which will guide us on the beautiful journey back home to which we have came from. Be still and know. I have helped many achieve the life they thought was impossible, they received this through inner work, changing the way they see things, loving themselves, living joy, healing from the past, releasing anger and believing that anything is possible. What I find happens to people is that when they receive what they have dreamt of they unknowingly disconnect from what they had once practiced and in turn bring their focus to the outside whether that's material or people. The new home they have received the partner they have wished for the new friends the holidays abroad. It becomes easier for all of their new fangled objects, events, experiences to bring them that feeing they desire, they become comfortable, it's easier for the food and the new partner to bring them the love they desire, their happiness becomes heavily reliant on the outside manifestation. One person said 'I have received all I wanted so I just stopped on my practices I had done to get there' The old beliefs and hurts start creeping back in again and they question why they are feeling like this when they have all they desired. We question why some of the rich and famous lives spiral out of control when they have so much that we would love to have. These are only material objects people keep wanting and searching for more to maintain a certain feeling, but you will never reach that feeling from anything outside of you we must stay connected, we must take time each day to give thanks, to be in silence without distraction, to do what makes our hearts sing and to meditate. A lot of people will find meditation in different ways, but whatever way you find is good for you just think of it as making your one phone call home that day. Speak with your mind and feel with your heart. Ask for your guidance and when you do this people will enter your life to help you. Every single person is on their own journey they will enter your life for a certain period some stay longer than others. Some are connected through a random conversation, some could be homeless on the street but know each and every person has their own journey and when it's their time to leave your path send them on their way with love no matter what has previously taken place. We are all here to expand our consciousness, to learn, to grow and sometimes it takes many people many life times to learn all of this. It is not my or your duty to interfere, we can be there for support and if they ask for help but we cannot force our thinking onto them 'if only you would do this' 'if only you would listen to me'

You are the most beautiful creation, you are a miracle, you are not here by accident, try to remember who you are. Who I AM Becoming. You will find this in your stillness and in peace. Take time each day to reconnect, in nature, in your office, by yourself, waiting in the car for the children coming from school. If you can make time to telephone or text or go on social media you can make time to connect to that one divine energy that will guide, protect, love and provide for you on this earthly plain. Life will become effortless. I sat with a group of business men and read the chapter 'being at peace' after reading I looked at their faces and saw that peace had descended upon each of them, even for just a short period. Each man had troubles in life even though they all had different stories to share each had two common denominators. One was that every trouble was fear based, someone had a client who had not paid rent on a commercial property he was fully aware of the energy and time he had spent chasing this client through emails, text messages and telephone calls. He was physically and mentally exhausted. The other had an ongoing issue with the bank and his property. Physically and mentally drained but was not prepared to let go of the frustration he held towards them, his belief *it's the principal of the matter*. One man shared how he would awaken each morning at 4am as would the constant array of negative thoughts of what had to be done, the lack of money which inevitably would continue throughout his day. The other common denominator was no man spent time in the morning or night to be in their silence. To connect their heart to that Divine Energy. There was no gratitude echoed in the still of the night or no positive intentions as the sun arose. One man said he would say prayers while driving to work in his car to his understanding this was enough and that was all he had time for. When you are driving you are not fully engaged with your intention, your gratitude or your heart. Your mind is switched on for pedestrians, other vehicles, traffic lights it's not possible to be fully engaged in your presence with so much focus for the mind taking place, you are simply rhyming of words in your prayer with no feeling. It is the feeling that is the prayer. Another shared that he would pray to his favourite saint before closing his eyes but still awoke with the negative thoughts. It didn't matter who he prayed to his true belief was that every day the sh*t would commence at 4am and continue until he closed his eyes and even then it would carry on into his sleep. What you believe and what you feel will be your truth. The truth is that if you deny yourself some precious time in the morning with your mobile phone switched off, even if it is just five minutes to take a few deep breaths, give gratitude for the perfection you are, what you have and the wonderful day that lies waiting you are denying yourself your truth. You are denying what you are, you are denying your creator the one thing you take for granted and that is your time. When we hold onto fears, worries, principals, righteousness we completely block of what we seek to receive. It's all very simple just take time in silence, hand over your worries, give gratitude for what you wish to receive, send love to those which you believe are causing you trouble, ask for all issues to be resolved for the highest good of everyone, your way is not the only way you just choose to believe it is. Let go of having to control people and outcomes, let go of feeling disrespected, let go of having to be right and proving your point. You are the one that is causing all of your problems and you are the one that can bring back your peace.

# *Remember*

Why do you not trust or believe in me? I have always been with you even before you came to this world. You are my most precious creation try today and see me in your reflection. Try today to see me on the frosty white trees, try today to hear me in the laughter, try today to see me in the grey of the cloud and ray of the sun. Even in your panic, fear, worry, sadness & loneliness I am more with you but you can't reach me. If you are feeling like this today my personal number is

...2 feet on the floor 1 hand on your heart 1 slow deep breath 1 slow deep breath 1 slow deep breath you may find connection is much better in quietness and stillness you will hear me better. There is no automated service just ask the question and you will hear my reply it may be in your head and yes it is me not you making up stuff or perhaps I will send a private messenger so watch out for them but either way just be clear about your concerns and ask the clear question for a clear answer. It's perfectly okay to ask me for a good life why would you be here for a miserable one? And please believe that even though in the human sense sometimes happenings don't make much sense but everything is in divine order, I have sent the most beautiful light workers to this earth to share with you their stories. Remember your spirit, remember who you are. I Am That I Am.

### *In a world of infinite possibilities*

### *what will you choose?*

*'To be a hostage to your ego on the red platform, or a host to God on the green platform'* – Declan Coyle

Love & Light

*Evelyn. x*

EVELYN MCALEER

Printed in Great Britain
by Amazon